BACK ROADS
TO F...

Books by Lawrence Ferlinghetti

BACK ROADS TO FAR PLACES

FERLINGHETTI

A NEW DIRECTIONS BOOK

New Directions Books are published for James Laughlin
by New Directions Publishing Corporation
333 Sixth Avenue, New York 10014.

for
Julie
on her way

BACK ROADS TO FAR PLACES

Let my
Japanese Pen tel its story

They say it is made
of bamboo shoot
does not scatter and
drops of black blood
when shaken
You have to put its foot down
right in the snow
before it will
walk off......•──•──•

The sun the sun the houses
of dawn the winterbirds
full of silence

No smoke rises
A single fan floats in the sky
over a boat offshore

I shoot it down
with an arrow
from Japan

Bashō would have liked
a lake like this
back roads
                    to far towns
reflected in it

West
Tree
Chest
Nut in foliage

Sun hung in it !

Sun sun
great god sun
becomes an oriental
every
day

As morning

mocks its flowers

by becoming

Afternoon

For we have
our moments of
ecstasy

and then
the *bird*

falls into
the absurd

And when the white furze
stands up
on the dandelion stem
it is time
to blow

O man in saffron
           in the Golden Gate
chanting Hare Krishna
       squatting lotus
           among the fern-fronds

At sundown
               no more Krishna

The fern-fronds
           unrolled !

Ah day is done
Day
is done
And fish float
through the trees
eating the seeds
of the sun

We were born
under the mulberry trees
from which drop
the mynah birds
of madness

Black rooks
like clouds
       of burnt paper
flowing through

       the skies

And the wind the wind
hides itself
in a hollow tree
And whistles out
at me

A million wild green seahorses
   shake out their
            white manes forever
on the Beach of the
          Small Round Stones

Will the world
   ever change?

On another far strand
dakinis in bikinis—

And there was light

where there
was flesh

Back on Bixby Beach
contemplating divine examples
of free will—
polliwogs
willing to lose
their tails

O listen
  to the sound of the sea
        my son

There is a fish in us
  who hears the ocean's
    long withdrawing Om

And echoes it

Looking for food + my father
I passed my third birthday
in a deserted kitchen
scanning cookbooks
written by men

Later
    I took up walking
and took steps
       to rectify
my earlier asininities

   Only to add to
       my hungers

And 'in the middle of the journey'
of my life
came upon my self

'in a dark wood'
And laughed + cried + lived + died

And understood Nothing

So like Nanao
in my old age
I'll be a strange/wild
wandering old man
thought by some
to be a sage
but also
just lost
in the dense wood
of the world

O leaf with Rama writ upon it !

On that 'continent of the spirit'
    just beyond
        the tip of my nose
I see the dark door

Sunlight casts its leaves
upon the wall
Wind stirs them
even
in the closed
room

Papyrus and bamboo
in the window's weather—
East + West's leaves
tangled together

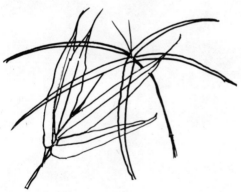

Outside
    a winter wind —

Some leaves
Fly by like birds

beaks
    blown away

Time a traveler
melting in eternity
(the mind coming and going)

Wash out your ears
with snow!

High upon Mount Tamal-fuji
came upon
a stone vagina—
Stone phallus
stuck in it
makes earth
quake

And in the hills in winter
took a bath in a hot spring
thinking of
the endless
muddy roads
of the Bolinas mesa
Pulled a plug
and drained it
To find the fish with golden eyes

Passing by
the roadside image
of some god
I fall
from my
sacred cow
into Nothingness

Ah how my life runs on
into the Real

back roads
    to far places

lost in the traces

What is that
strange sense of yearning
passing
lighted houses
at night

?

loneliness
sets its own lamp
alight

Last night a longing

        a roaring in a sea shell

  a confused murmur

        of birds + men

And bodies

        were boats

Hull of flesh with nine holes
I float down
        the roaring stream
And the water
                light

A flutter of wings
Sound and weeping
fill the air
And the quivering
meat wheel
turns

O wheel of meat
made of us
with no end and no beginning
(all beings being one)

turn and turn and turn!

Upon that tree of heaven
that sprang up out of the sea
and over-arched the skies
hanging by our teeth
with no other Answer

142588

I ask myself just wherein lieth
that source of inner joy
while all outside dieth
in charcoal night

The source is life itself

The source is sun

The source is light

Yes wake o wake
for the sun that riseth
with the rising wind
will all too soon
o all too soon
our turning World consume

But the mind
the mind also rises
And still the jetsun shines
                    and shines
And still the sea
            sighs its answer
its 'full account
          of Om'

The door to the invisible
is visible
The hidden door
is not hidden
I walk through it forever
not seeing it
I am what I am
And will be
what I will be

So passing strange mountains

And dropping pine needles

in an envelope

I send you
some of my

bones